kids draw™

FUNNY & SPOOKY HOLIDAY CHARACTERS

CHRISTOPHER HART

WATSON-GUPTILL PUBLICATIONS/NEW YORK

For my dad, Stan Hart

Senior Editor: Candace Raney
Editors: Alisa Palazzo and Julie Mazur
Designers: Bob Fillie, Graphiti Design, Inc. and Cheryl Viker
Production Manager: Hector Campbell

Cover art by Christopher Hart
Text copyright © 2001 Christopher Hart
Illustrations copyright © 1999 Christopher Hart

First published in 2001 by
Watson-Guptill Publications,
a division of BPI Communications, Inc.,
770 Broadway, New York, N.Y. 10003
www.watsonguptill.com

Based on *How to Draw Halloween, Christmas & Seasonal Characters,*
first published by Watson-Guptill Publications in 1999

Library of Congress Card Number: 00-111777

Printed in Singapore

First printing, 2001

1 2 3 4 5 6 7 8 / 08 07 06 05 04 03 02 01

CONTENTS

INTRODUCTION

This is a monster of a book—funny monsters, that is. Every wacky monster to ever haunt a house is here: vampires, ghosts, goblins, mummies, devils, zombies, witches, hunchbacks, and more. It's good ghoulish fun as you learn to draw your favorite creepy creep!

From there, we turn our sights to the enchanted winter scenes of Christmas, with characters like Santa and Mrs. Claus, Rudolph and the reindeer, snow fairies, and of course those hardworking elves. You'll also learn how to draw fun characters for other holidays, from Cupid for Valentine's Day to leprechauns for St. Patrick's Day, black cats for Friday the 13th, and many more!

The book begins with a quick look at some basic art principles, like body movement, line flow, and how using overlapping shapes will make your characters look real. Best of all, you'll learn to create original cartoon characters of your very own!

Holidays give us fun throughout the year. Whether you want to improve your drawing skills or create a project for your family or class, this book is for you!

BASIC POINTERS 'N' STUFF

Let's start with a few basic principles of drawing. Try to remember these as you work through the book.

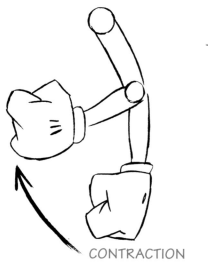

CONTRACTION

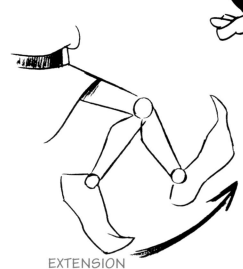

EXTENSION

ROTATION

BENDING

How the Body Moves

We all have joints in our bodies that allow us to move. Let's take your basic elf as an example. The major joints are at the waist, shoulders, elbows, wrists, knees, ankles, and neck. Here are the four basic ways the body moves.

Oh, You Devil!

Start with a sneaky-looking human. Then give him a small beard and a trim little mustache. Add pointed ears, horns, and a pointed tail. Draw a long cape with a high collar, and put a pitchfork in his hand.

THE EVIL SMILE
Almost all Halloween characters have one thing in common: an evil smile. There's a sense of glee in their wickedness, because these bad guys are all nuts!

Zombies

Zombies are dead men and women who have risen out of their graves in search of people to terrify. They wear the clothes they were buried in, which are by now pretty tattered. They walk stiffly and don't look too healthy, either. Their eyes stare without blinking, so make the eyeballs large and round.

Windy graveyards are great haunts for the haunted. To draw wind, show how it affects things like clothing, hair, and weeds. Everything should blow in the same direction.

Draw a hunchback with the back much higher than the head. The arms should be on the thin side. One famous hunchback is Quasimodo, a character in a book by Victor Hugo called *The Hunchback of Notre Dame*.

Mr. Hyde

Dr. Jekyll is a character in Robert Louis Stevenson's book *Dr. Jekyll and Mr. Hyde.* The story takes place in old London, England. Dr. Jekyll transforms himself from a caring doctor into a wicked, soulless villain—Mr. Hyde. Mr. Hyde sports a top hat and a cape. He has large jowls, bushy eyebrows, and a heavy forehead. Be sure to add ragged hair and thick fingers with pointed nails. And most importantly, give him a bent, cowardly posture.

OWL

Spooky, Creepy, and Icky

Here are more characters and decorations you can use to liven up a good Halloween drawing.

CRESCENT MOON

SKELETON

MASK

BOO!

GHOST

CANDELABRA

JACK-O'-LANTERN

The Classic Haunted House

Haunted houses need to be falling apart and should be located right next to a cemetery. (Location, location, location!) There's usually a rusty old fence at the entrance, and the stairs leading up to the front door are missing slats. A weather vane crowns the house. A full moon hangs in the sky, and at least one leafless, twisted tree should be close by. You shouldn't be able to see anything through the dark windows except for curtains—or maybe shadows.

Haunted Mansions

Warm and cozy, ain't it? Witches and ghosts live in haunted houses, but devils and vampires have haunted *mansions* or castles (see page 16). The ceilings of haunted mansions must be very high. This makes the "guests" feel vulnerable. To show this, draw the scene from a high angle, looking down on the people.

CHRISTMAS CHARACTERS

Once December comes, you can't pass a store without seeing Christmas characters. Cartoonists work hard to bring these characters to life. Let's discover their secrets and learn how to draw them ourselves!

Santa Claus

Since Santa always has a big beard, just include the shape of the beard into the basic structure of his face. Draw the mouth first, then draw the mustache on top of it.

Ruffles go on the underside of the mustache.

"Santa's Workshop"
Elves love catching Santa secretly
enjoying one of their new inventions
when he thinks no one is watching.

"Special Delivery"
Rooftop scenes are important for any good Christmas story.

"Stuck in the Chimney"
It's too late to think about dieting now!

"The Day After Christmas"
Santa's round body, classic beard, and mustache make him easy to recognize, even without his red suit.

47

A Christmas Carol

Charles Dickens' story *A Christmas Carol* features many well-known characters, such as Ebenezer Scrooge. Scrooge learned that getting isn't as important to happiness as giving.

Notice the funny bump on the back of his head.

SCROOGE
Give Scrooge thin arms and legs, and hunch his shoulders a bit.

GHOST OF JACOB MARLEY
Tilt him slightly so that he looks like he's floating. Keep his arms down by his sides to make him seem weak.

Christmas Carolers

To show people singing, draw them with their mouths opened wide, their heads tilted, and their eyes shut. Notice that here I made the smallest girl different. Her eyes are wide open, her head is straight, and her mouth is open only a little bit. Variety makes things more interesting.

The Nutcracker

The Nutcracker is *the* Christmas ballet, performed each year for kids who beg their parents to let them stay home and watch cartoons instead. (My parents didn't listen to me, either.) In this story, toy nutcrackers are really little soldiers. They carry fancy swords and are dressed with lots of flair and pomp. The platform under the soldier makes him look like a toy.

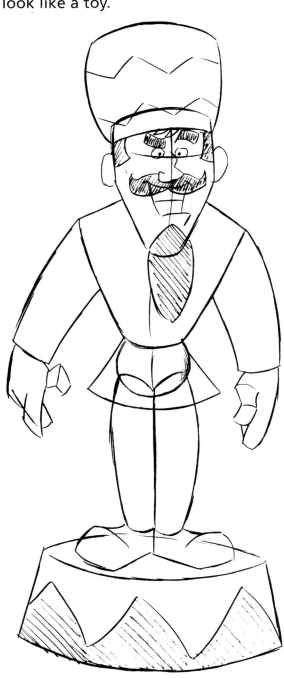

Christmas Ballerina

Here's a Christmas ballerina for you to practice.

STRETCH
You can feel her stretch as she arches every part of her body.

TWIST
Her hips twist to the left while her upper body twists to the right. This makes the pose more dynamic.

LINE FLOW
A single line flows from her right toe all the way up her body, finishing under her left arm.

Snow Fairies

Snow fairies are tiny beings who sprinkle the first frost over hills, trees, and towns. Draw them with large heads and thin bodies to make them seem light. Add gentle wings and antennae. Snow fairies are really just cute little elves with a few bug parts.

Different Types of Christmas Trees

You can draw Christmas trees in many different ways.

CLASSIC

NEAT & TRIM

SHAGGY

CONE-SHAPED

WREATH WITH RIBBON
Wreaths are also popular at Christmas.

OTHER HOLIDAYS AND OCCASIONS

There are lots of fun holidays, from Thanksgiving to Easter and everything in between.

Thanksgiving

Thanksgiving is an American holiday that goes back to the time of the Pilgrims. We celebrate it with food and decorations that remind us of those times.

Gobble Gobble

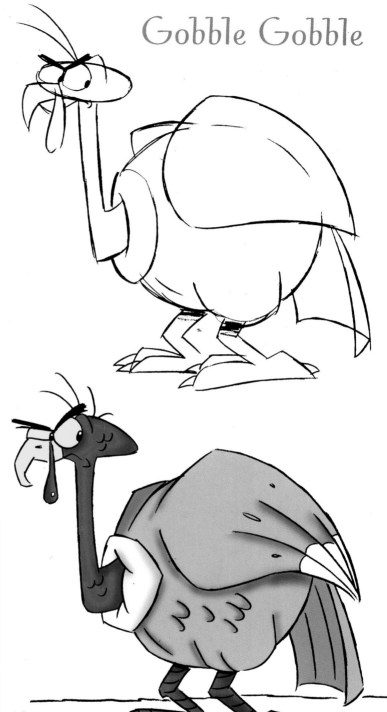

The turkey is one incredibly ugly bird. Its neck and head are scaly. Its body is plump and awkward. It has that weird thingy hanging from its beak. And its legs look worse than your grandmother's. I'm talking ugly!

Pilgrims

Pilgrims wore sturdy clothes in grays, blacks, and browns. No lime-green jackets or polka-dotted skirts here.

PILGRIM KIDS
Pilgrim children were dressed as formally as their parents.

Easter

The Easter bunny has buck teeth, a bushy tail, and long ears. Don't forget to add extra-long feet, bushy cheeks, and whiskers, too.

The muzzle (mouth area) is shaped like a kidney bean.

More Easter Rabbits

This rabbit's hands drag behind him as he pulls the heavy sack.

WORK, WORK, WORK
Hauling Easter eggs is a tough job, but someone's gotta do it. Draw this guy a bit thin—just look at the exercise he's getting!

THE BUSINESSMAN
For this rabbit, everything's strictly business. Draw one flat eyebrow across both eyes. Then hide the pupils halfway underneath it.

HAPPY BUNNY
Don't leave out the bounce line behind this joyful bunny.

BROKEN EGGS 1¢

The Easter Chick

There aren't many things cuter than a little chick. People often buy chicks for Easter, forgetting that the chicks soon grow up to be chickens. And there are lots of things cuter than chickens.

FRONT VIEW WITH BASIC CONSTRUCTION

SIDE VIEW

DECORATIVE EASTER EGGS
Try to invent
your own patterns.

3/4 VIEW

St. Patrick's Day

LEPRECHAUNS

Leprechauns have pots of gold stashed somewhere in the woods, but they won't tell where. They're little people who always dress in green, have beards, and wear short, round hats with buckles.

To create a dynamic pose, start your drawing with a sweeping line of action.

The way a character runs should be a reflection of his or her personality. This leprechaun's run is much more carefree than that of the guy chasing him.

Leprechauns are very hard to catch. If caught, they must reveal the location of their hidden treasure.

Valentine's Day

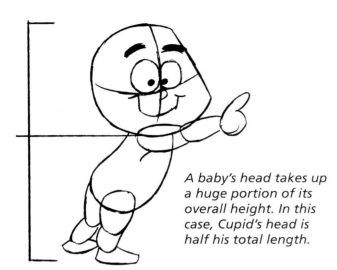

A baby's head takes up a huge portion of its overall height. In this case, Cupid's head is half his total length.

CUPID
Cupid is a chubby baby boy with wings. Give him curly hair and a twinkle in his eye. His legs and tummy must be pudgy, and his eyes should be big.

Groundhog Day

The groundhog hibernates in its burrow all winter. Then, as legend has it, it opens its eyes on February 2 and pokes its head out to see if it's spring yet. If the groundhog can see its own shadow, there'll be six more weeks of winter. If not, spring is almost here.

THE GROUNDHOG
I like to give the groundhog pajamas. It's also important to add big buck teeth and short little whiskers, plus tiny ears and bushy cheeks.

Friday the 13th

On Friday the 13th, people watch out for signs of bad luck.

THE BLACK CAT
The most popular symbol of bad luck is the black cat. If a black cat crosses your path, you're in for it. This cat should be sneaky. Having it walk on tiptoes gives it a silly, sinister quality.

INDEX